Pebble®
Plus

Look Inside Animal Homes
Look Inside an Ant Nest

by Megan Cooley Peterson

Consulting Editor: Gail Saunders-Smith, PhD

Consultant: Laura Jesse, PhD
Iowa State University Extension

CAPSTONE PRESS
a capstone imprint

Pebble Plus is published by Capstone Press,
1710 Roe Crest Drive, North Mankato, Minnesota 56003.
www.capstonepub.com

 Books published by Capstone Press are manufactured with paper
containing at least 10 percent post-consumer waste.

Library of Congress Cataloging-in-Publication Data
Peterson, Megan Cooley.
  Look inside an ant nest / by Megan Cooley Peterson.
    p. cm.—(Pebble plus. Look inside animal homes)
  Includes bibliographical references and index.
  Summary: "Full-color photographs and simple text describe ant nests"—Provided by publisher.
  ISBN 978-1-4296-6078-5 (library binding)
  1. Ants—Habitations—Juvenile literature. 2. Ant communities—Juvenile literature. I. Title.
  QL568.F7P45 2012
  595.79'61782—dc22   2011000266

Editorial Credits
Katy Kudela, editor; Gene Bentdahl, designer; Marcie Spence, media researcher; Laura Manthe, production specialist

Photo Credits
Alamy Images: blickwinkel, 5, 17, Daniel L. Geiger/SNAP, 7; iStockphoto: Cabezonication, cover, 15; Minden Pictures:
Mark Moffett, 19; photolibrary/Peter Arnold: KBogon, 11; Shutterstock: Henrik Larsson, 13, 21, Steve Shoup, 1;
Visuals Unlimited: Alex Wild, 9

Note to Parents and Teachers

The Look Inside Animal Homes series supports national science standards related to life
science. This book describes and illustrates ant nests. The images support early readers in
understanding the text. The repetition of words and phrases helps early readers learn new
words. This book also introduces early readers to subject-specific vocabulary words, which are
defined in the Glossary section. Early readers may need assistance to read some words and to
use the Table of Contents, Glossary, Read More, Internet Sites, and Index sections of the book.

Printed in the United States of America in North Mankato, Minnesota.
012012   006536CGVMI

Table of Contents

A Home for Ants

Most ant colonies live
in nests all year long.
One nest might hold
hundreds, thousands,
or even millions of ants.

Building an Ant Nest

Worker ants build nests

almost everywhere on Earth.

They build nests in wood

or in soil. Some ants build

nests out of leaves and silk.

Many ant nests take
weeks or months to build.
Worker ants first dig tunnels
underground or inside trees.

Worker ants build chambers

inside the tunnels.

Some nests have only

a few chambers. Other nests

have thousands of rooms.

Some ants pile soil and twigs on top of the nest. They dig tunnels and rooms inside the pile. Some piles reach 5 feet (1.5 meters) tall.

Inside an Ant Nest

A small opening lets ants

into the nest.

Guard ants keep out enemies.

They may sting, bite,

or spray poison.

The queen ant lays eggs
in some of the chambers.
Queens lay up to 1,000 eggs
a day. Worker ants take
care of the eggs and young.

queen ant

Worker ants store food in some chambers. Ants eat seeds, nectar, and other insects. Some ants grow fungi inside the nest for food.

fungus garden

In spring or summer, a
young queen ant starts a
new colony. She lays eggs.
The eggs hatch, and young
worker ants build a new nest.

Glossary

chamber—a room in an ant nest

colony—a group of animals that live together

fungus—a living thing similar to a plant but without flowers, leaves, or green coloring

hatch—to break out of an egg

nectar—a sweet liquid found in many flowers

poison—a substance that can kill or harm a person, animal, or plant

queen ant—an adult female ant that lays eggs; most colonies have only one queen ant

silk—a sticky fiber made by some ants

soil—dirt or earth in which plants grow

worker ant—an adult female ant that does not lay eggs; worker ants build nests and take care of young ants

Read More

Rustad, Martha E. H. *Ants and Aphids Work Together.* Animals Working Together. Mankato, Minn.: Capstone Press, 2011.

Stewart, Melissa. *Ants.* National Geographic Readers: Level 1. Washington, D.C.: National Geographic, 2010.

Internet Sites

FactHound offers a safe, fun way to find Internet sites related to this book. All of the sites on FactHound have been researched by our staff.

Here's all you do:

Visit *www.facthound.com*

Type in this code: 9781429660785

Super-cool stuff! Check out projects, games and lots more at **www.capstonekids.com**

Index

Word Count: 206
Grade: 1
Early-Intervention Level: 14

24